Published in Nashville, Tennessee, by Tommy Nelson™, a division of Thomas Nelson, Inc.
Vice President of Children's Books: Laura Minchew; Project Manager: Karen Gallini; Editor: Tama Fortner

Designed by Koechel Peterson & Associates

Scripture is taken from the *New King James Version*. Copyright © 1982 by Thomas Nelson, Inc. Used by
permission. All rights reserved. Scriptures followed by ICB are quoted from the *International Children's Bible,
New Century Version*, copyright © 1986, 1988 by Word Publishing, Nashville, Tennessee. Used by permission.

ISBN 0-8499-5912-8

Printed in the United States of America
99 00 01 02 03 RRD 9 8 7 6 5 4 3

Thomas
Kinkade

Grandfather's Memories
TO HIS GRANDCHILD

Featuring the art of THOMAS KINKADE

Written by Candy Paull

Tommy NELSON

Thomas Nelson, Inc.
Nashville

To the Reader:

I think grandfathers are extraordinary people. They offer their grandchildren love, patience, understanding—and more love.

Growing up, I did not have the opportunity to see my grandparents as much as I would have liked. I do remember that one of my grandfathers had a big shock of white hair, and he was missing a finger, which fascinated my brother and me. As it turned out, my grandfather had owned his own meat company in St. Louis. He was also a butcher, and he had lost his finger in an accident while at work. He loved all kinds of food, and when my mother prepared for him a favorite casserole, he bubbled over with excitement. (And loosened his belt a notch or two when the meal was over.) I remember that when he and my grandmother took my brother and me for a walk, they talked with us and really listened to us. The big, white-haired gentleman even bent laboriously over so we could whisper in his ear.

Your grandfather must love you very much. It takes a lot of time and thought to complete this journal, to share stories and family history and dreams. I imagine that if you read these pages carefully, you will find that not only is your grandfather a fascinating person, but you may be more like him than you think.

In Psalm 78:1–4, the Bible says,

> My people, listen to my teaching. Listen to what I say. I will speak using stories. I will tell things that have been secret since long ago. We have heard them and know them. Our fathers told them to us. We will not keep them from our children. We will tell those who come later about the praise of the LORD. We will tell about His power and the miracles He has done. (ICB)

This is what your grandfather has done for you with this journal. It is my hope that the words and paintings in this journal bring you closer to your grandfather and to our Heavenly Father.

Dearest Grandchild,

This journal is my gift to you. I have filled it with my thoughts,

memories, and hopes for the future. I have written in these pages

about the things that I did growing up and the things I learned,

as well as the person I have become. I hope it helps you understand

who I am. The legacy that I want to pass on to you is the precious

gift of faith, a heritage of love of God and love of family that

you can one day give to your own grandchildren.

I thank God every day for you and pray that this journal

will remind you always of how much your grandfather loves you.

Always,

For whatever is born of God overcomes the world. And this is the victory that has overcome the world—our faith.

1 JOHN 5:4

MY BIRTH

My full name

I was given this name because

My birth date and the place where I was born

Who took care of me when I was a child

My earliest memory

For You are my rock and my fortress; therefore,
for Your name's sake, lead me and guide me.

PSALM 31:3

What was happening in the world when I was born

The president of the United States when I was born

ABOUT MY MOTHER,
Your Great~Grandmother

My mother's full maiden name

_____

_____

Her birth date and place of birth

_____

_____

My mother's best story about growing up

_____

_____

_____

_____

My favorite memory of my mother

_____

_____

_____

_____

_____

_____

_____

ABOUT MY FATHER,
Your Great-Grandfather

My father's full name

His birth date and place of birth

My father's best story about growing up

My favorite memory of my father

Honor your father and your mother.

EXODUS 20:12

MY FAMILY

My brothers' and sisters' names

How we got along

Our biggest argument

The games we played as children

Now that we are all grown up

For this reason I bow my knees to the Father of our Lord Jesus Christ,
from whom the whole family in heaven and earth is named.

EPHESIANS 3:14-15

A funny story about us

Our most memorable family reunion

ME

My greatest strength

My greatest weakness

One thing I love to do

One thing I hate to do

The LORD is my strength and song, and He has become my salvation;
He is my God, and I will praise Him.

EXODUS 15:2

I always laugh when

When I look at the world, I see

MY CHILDHOOD HOME

One favorite memory of home

_____

_____

_____

_____

My parents made our house a home by

_____

_____

_____

_____

The yard I played in

_____
_____
_____
_____

Our next-door neighbors

_____
_____
_____
_____

My childhood bedroom

_____
_____
_____
_____

My favorite hiding place

_____
_____
_____
_____

My house shall be called a house
of prayer for all nations.
ISAIAH 56:7

MY HOMETOWN

The town where we lived

Where I played with my friends

Someone I respected in my hometown

My favorite store and why I loved to go there

You are the light of the world.
A city that is set on a hill cannot be hidden.

MATTHEW 5:14

The biggest event in our town was

The place where we worshiped

A TYPICAL DAY

My father worked at

During the day, my mother

A practical joke that I played or that was played on me

The chores I had to do

Let the little children come to Me, and do not forbid
them; for of such is the kingdom of heaven.

MATTHEW 19:14

On summer days, I liked to

On winter evenings, I enjoyed

MY FAVORITE SPORTS

My favorite sports

My greatest victory

My biggest sports defeat and how I overcame it

My father taught me

The sports that you and I enjoy together

But those who wait on the LORD shall renew their strength;
they shall mount up with wings like eagles,
they shall run and not be weary,
they shall walk and not faint.

ISAIAH 40:31

WHEN I WAS A BOY

What an ice cream cone cost when I was young

What an ice cream cone costs today

The kind of car we drove

How people dressed

But as many as received Him, to them He gave
the right to become children of God.

JOHN 1:12

How boys were expected to behave

The most exciting invention at the time

MY PETS

My first pet

My favorite pet

The animal that makes the best pet and why

The different kinds of pets I have owned

Out of the ground the LORD *God formed every beast of the field and every bird of the air, and brought them to Adam to see what he would call them.*

GENESIS 2:19

I always wanted a

_____

_____

Some of my pets' names

_____

_____

_____

_____

_____

SPIRITUAL BEGINNINGS

The first person who told me about God

_____

_____

_____

_____

My first Communion

_____

_____

_____

_____

My favorite person from the Bible

_____

_____

_____

_____

The first time I knew God was real

_____

_____

_____

_____

_____

Behold what manner of love the Father has bestowed
on us, that we should be called children of God!

1 JOHN 3:1

A time I had to stand up for my beliefs

How my beliefs have changed since I was a child

My Favorite Verse as a Child

WITH MY FATHER
Your Great-Grandfather

The most wonderful thing about my father

My father was especially good at

My father let me "help" by

A wise son makes a glad father.

PROVERBS 10:1

My father wanted me to be

The things my father taught me about God

WITH MY MOTHER
Your Great-Grandmother

The most wonderful thing about my mother

My mother was especially good at

She encouraged me to

Lessons I learned from my mother

She opens her mouth with wisdom,
and on her tongue is the law of kindness.

PROVERBS 31:26

The sweetest memory of my mother

_____

_____

_____

_____

The things my mother taught me about God

_____

_____

_____

_____

EARLY SCHOOL YEARS

The school I attended

My favorite teacher and why

My least favorite teacher and why

My best and worst subjects in school

The friends I played with after school

The after-school activities I was involved in

A school event I will never forget

Learn to do good.
ISAIAH 1:17

HIGH SCHOOL YEARS

The school I attended

My favorite teacher and why

My best subject and why

A coach I admired

For whatever things were written before were
written for our learning, that we through the patience
and comfort of the Scriptures might have hope.

ROMANS 15:4

A hero I wanted to be like when I was in high school

Popular fads when I was in high school

The friends I spent time with

MUSIC

Growing up, my favorite songs and musicians were

As I got older, I discovered

Now, I like to listen to

Music lessons or classes I took

Sing to the LORD a new song,
and His praise in the assembly of saints.

PSALM 149:1

My favorite hymn

Your grandmother's and my favorite song

FIRST TIMES

The first time I drove a car

When I got my driver's license

My first car

The first time I shaved

The first time I voted in an election

The first time I asked a girl for a date

You shall love the LORD your God with all your heart,
with all your soul, and with all your mind.
This is the first and great commandment.

MATTHEW 22:37-38

FRIENDSHIP

My closest friend when I was growing up

My best friend today

Being a friend means

You are not only my grandchild, you are also my friend because

A friend loves at all times.

PROVERBS 17:17

I have seen you be a friend when

God can be a friend when

MY FIRST ROMANCE

My first "crush"

_____

_____

_____

_____

_____

_____

My first girlfriend

_____

_____

_____

_____

_____

My first kiss

On dates, my girlfriend and I often went to

My heart was broken when

We love Him because He first loved us.

1 JOHN 4:19

JOURNEYS

The first time I rode a bike

The best vacation we had as a family

A favorite fishing, hiking, or camping trip

My first plane trip

I have always wanted to go

The most exciting trip I have ever taken

The first trip I took without my family

Be strong and of good courage . . . for the LORD
your God is with you wherever you go.

JOSHUA 1:9

SPIRITUAL LESSONS

Practicing your faith means

_____

_____

_____

_____

A real Christian

_____

_____

_____

_____

God seems especially close when

_____

_____

_____

_____

My favorite passage of Scripture

_____

_____

_____

_____

_____

Now faith is the substance of things hoped for,
the evidence of things not seen.

HEBREWS 11:1

Someone who teaches me about God now

One lesson I would like you to learn about faith

My Favorite Verse about Faith

GOALS

A goal I set and reached

My greatest fear

My biggest disappointment

Defeat can be turned into success when

My goals today

A goal that I was proud to see you achieve

*Let us lay aside every weight, and the sin which
so easily ensnares us, and let us run with endurance
the race that is set before us.*

HEBREWS 12:1

FALLING IN LOVE

I always thought that love was

_____

_____

_____

_____

God says that love is

_____

_____

_____

How old I was when I met your grandmother

_____

_____

_____

_____

Where we met

_____

_____

_____

_____

Though I have all faith, so that I could remove mountains,
but have not love, I am nothing.

1 CORINTHIANS 13:2

I was attracted to her because

_____

_____

_____

_____

_____

I proposed by

_____

_____

_____

_____

_____

MY WEDDING DAY

The place where we were married

The date and time when we were married

On our wedding day, your grandmother looked

The wedding ceremony made me feel

My best man was

The kind of wedding it was

My most vivid memory of our wedding

For our honeymoon, we went to

Live joyfully with the wife whom you love.

ECCLESIASTES 9:9

LIFE AS NEWLYWEDS

The first place we lived

_____

_____

_____

_____

One thing we still laugh about

_____

_____

_____

_____

The thing I love best about your grandmother

_____

_____

_____

_____

Our first fight

_____

_____

_____

_____

Love . . . bears all things, believes all things, hopes all things, endures all things.

1 CORINTHIANS 13:4, 7

The most important thing I have learned about being married

Where we worship

MY LIFE AS A FATHER

Our children, their names and birth dates

What I love about being a father

The most difficult thing a father has to do is

I would have been a better father if

One thing I learned from my children

An important lesson that I hope all my children and grandchildren learn

Train up a child in the way he should go,
and when he is old he will not depart from it.

PROVERBS 22:6

A PERSONAL FAITH

I know there is a God because

I experienced a turning point in my faith when

When times are difficult, I turn to

The best place for me to pray

And whatever things you ask in prayer, believing, you will receive.

MATTHEW 21:22

The best time for me to pray

When I die, I believe that

My Favorite Verse about God

YOUR MOTHER

Your mother's full maiden name

Her birth date and place of birth

The thing I love best about your mother

YOUR FATHER

Your father's full name

His birth date and place of birth

The thing I love best about your father

Beloved, let us love one another, for love is of God;
and everyone who loves is born of God and knows God.

1 JOHN 4:7

YOU

Your birth date and the place where you were born

_____

_____

_____

The first time I held you in my arms, I felt

_____

_____

_____

_____

The person in our family that you remind me of most

_____

_____

_____

_____

The first words you said to me

_____

_____

_____

_____

My Favorite Photo of You

PLACE
A FAVORITE
PHOTO HERE

I will praise You, for I am fearfully and wonderfully made.

MY DREAMS FOR YOU

The ways you are like me

The ways you are different from me

The ways you are like no one else in the world

Something I want you to remember about me when you grow up

Let no one despise your youth, but be an example to the believers in word,
in conduct, in love, in spirit, in faith, in purity.

1 TIMOTHY 4:12

You have the potential to

My dream for you

73

CELEBRATING CHRISTMAS

My childhood Christmases were like

Our family's favorite Christmas tradition

My best Christmas ever

The best Christmas gift

The real meaning of Christmas

At Christmas, our church

Glory to God in the highest, and on earth peace,
goodwill toward men!

LUKE 2:14

MY FAVORITE THINGS

My favorite books as a child

My favorite books as an adult

My favorite poem

A treasured memento from my boyhood

For where your treasure is, there your heart will be also.

MATTHEW 6:21

My favorite place to think

That which I value most in life

LOOKING AHEAD

The dearest people on earth

The people I miss most

I am happiest when I think of

_____

_____

_____

_____

I am most thankful for

_____

_____

_____

_____

If I could have anything, it would be

_____

_____

_____

_____

I wish for our family

_____

_____

_____

_____

_____

If they obey and serve Him, they shall spend their
days in prosperity, and their years in pleasures.

JOB 36:11

WINNING AT LIFE

I always wanted to

I think that real success means

You are only a failure if

I believe that you could

When you pass through the waters,
I will be with you.

ISAIAH 43:2

My dad taught me that winners always

I have seen you be a winner when

TIME WITH YOU

When I am with you, I like to

One funny memory I have of you

One sweet memory I have of you

_____

_____

_____

It is amazing to watch you

_____

_____

_____

As you get older, I would like to

_____

_____

_____

You have a great talent for

_____

_____

_____

_____

I thank my God upon every remembrance of you.

PHILIPPIANS 1:3

THE WORKING WORLD

My very first job

My first "real" job

My favorite kind of work

A typical day at my work

*All Scripture is given by inspiration of God . . .
that the man of God may be complete,
thoroughly equipped for every good work.*

2 TIMOTHY 3:16-17

What I do now

My advice to you about work

HOBBIES

My favorite hobby is

_____

_____

_____

_____

The person who first introduced me to this hobby

_____

_____

_____

_____

I have always wanted to try

_____

_____

_____

_____

I want to teach you how to

_____

_____

_____

_____

An important lesson I have learned from doing what I love

_____

_____

_____

_____

Something we both love to do together

_____

_____

_____

_____

Now may the God of hope fill you with all joy and peace in believing,
that you may abound in hope by the power of the Holy Spirit.

ROMANS 15:13

GROWING IN WISDOM

In my twenties, I thought I would

_____

_____

_____

_____

In my thirties, I became

_____

_____

_____

_____

In my forties, I wanted to

_____

_____

_____

_____

In my fifties, I discovered

_____

_____

_____

_____

_____

All Your works shall praise You, O LORD,
and Your saints shall bless You.

PSALM 145:10

Now that I'm a grandfather

Major milestones in my life include

Being a grandfather means

_____

_____

_____

_____

_____

The best thing about being your grandfather

_____

_____

_____

_____

_____

90

When you have a grandchild, be sure to

Teach your grandchild

A grandchild is

Remember to tell your grandchild

Behold, children are a heritage from the LORD.

PSALM 127:3

My Favorite Verse about Life

OUR FAMILY

Our Family Tree

Maternal Great-Grandmother
_____
Date of Birth (death)
_____
Marriage

Maternal Great-Grandfather
_____
Date of Birth (death)

Maternal Great-Grandmother
_____
Date of Birth (death)
_____
Marriage

Maternal Great-Grandfather
_____
Date of Birth (death)

Paternal Great-Grandmother
_____
Date of Birth (death)
_____
Marriage

Paternal Great-Grandfather
_____
Date of Birth (death)

Paternal Great-Grandmother
_____
Date of Birth (death)
_____
Marriage

Paternal Great-Grandfather
_____
Date of Birth (death)

Your Grandmother
_____
Date of Birth (death)
_____
Marriage

Your Grandfather
_____
Date of Birth (death)

Your Grandmother
_____
Date of Birth (death)
_____
Marriage

Your Grandfather
_____
Date of Birth (death)

Your Mother
_____
Date of Birth (death)
_____
Marriage

Your Father
_____
Date of Birth (death)

You
_____
Date of Birth

Your Sibling
_____
Date of Birth

Your Sibling
_____
Date of Birth

Your Sibling
_____
Date of Birth

Your Sibling
_____
Date of Birth

A Favorite Photo of You and Me

PLACE
A FAVORITE
PHOTO HERE

Blessed be the LORD God of Israel from everlasting to everlasting!
And let all the people say, "Amen!"

PSALM 106:48

INDEX OF PAINTINGS